TOILET TRAIN[

AUTISTIC & SEND

CHILDREN AND ADULTS

A step-by-step guide for parents, carers, and professionals to toilet-train children and adults with autism and other disabilities

By

Faria Arsh

ISBN: 978-969-3192-36-0

Table of Contents

Acknowledgments

I would like to extend my gratitude to my parents, Fariduddin Shaik Imam and Azra Imam. They have loved me unconditionally and supported me throughout my life at every step. I have named my business after my mum to honour her support and her sacrifices for me. I am thankful to my siblings Maheen Shaik Imam and Moinuddin Almas Imam for their unwavering support that helps me to achieve anything I want. They love both my girls like their own and I couldn't ask for better siblings. It goes without saying that my family has helped me a lot with Afiyah.

Faiza, my firstborn, and what a marvelous young lady she has turned into. Those who have seen her with Afiyah will agree she has played the role of a young carer out of her own will and without any hesitation.

I am truly grateful to Bernie for supporting Afiyah, Faiza, and me for over 10 years and counting. She has helped us through Afiyah's diagnosis, various behavioural challenges, and the toilet training process. Bernie also provided me with a great deal of emotional support when needed.

I would like to thank my best friend Sheila for always being there for us, picking up prescriptions for Afiyah at short notice, coming to visit us when we were alone and much more.

I am thankful to my kind friend Janine McDonald for recognising my efforts in supporting other families in need and nominating me for the SHEro award at The She Inspires Awards.

I have had the privilege of working with amazing colleagues at Pictor Academy and some of them have helped me with Afiyah's behavioural difficulties, communication, and brainstormed toilet training strategies. I will always be grateful to them: Jacqueline Wheble, Kerry Butler, Catherine Colligan, Karen Massey, Kaye Harwood, Beverley Owens, Carmen Gornal and Sean Cusack.

I wouldn't have managed to come this far without all the people I've mentioned in this book.

Last but not the least, the star of the book, Afiyah. Those who know Afiyah will agree, despite the challenges she faces every day; she brings a smile to everyone's face and has the most infectious laughter. Without her, I wouldn't be writing this book.

About the Author

Faria Arsh is a single mother of two teenage girls, Faiza, 18, and Afiyah, 15. Afiyah was diagnosed with autism at the age of 3 and since then also has had a diagnosis of ADHD, severe learning difficulties, and epilepsy. Faria has always been extremely passionate about learning about autism and supporting other families too. She has worked as a Specialist Teaching Assistant at an outstanding special school for several years but gave up her career due to her caring needs for her children, especially Afiyah. Faria's main interests are in autism, communication, and behavioural analysis. With those skills combined, she has put together a unique toilet-training program that has helped her daughter Afiyah and also helped other children from her work at the special school. This is a behavioural toilet-training program, and it can be used for all age groups and abilities. Other parents relate to Faria because they feel Faria has a deeper understanding of autism and the everyday difficulties autism families go through. Faria is currently an enterprising entrepreneur working from home, so she can work around Afiyah's needs and be available for both of her children. She makes soy candles, soaps, and other products, and everything in her store is vegan and eco-friendly. Although she doesn't work at the special school anymore, she is still in touch with various parents who have autistic children and other disabilities so that she can offer her support to them when needed. Faria runs a Facebook page called Living_With_Autism, where she regularly shares information, ideas, and facts about Afiyah's life to raise awareness about autism. Faria has been invited to run communication and toilet training workshops for parents. Recently Faria has also started raising awareness about the difficulties parents and carers go through and the bias they are subjected to by people within their family, friends circle, and professionals. Faria wants to raise awareness so that families who have children with additional needs feel supported by the community. Faria understands the importance of a good support network and the positive difference it can bring to anyone going through difficulties. Although Faria's parents and siblings live abroad and her mum visits Faria frequently to help, Faria says their moral support, kind words, and love is all she needs. Faria has now also surrounded herself with friends who are kind and supportive of her and her children and urges all parents/carers to do the same. She hopes to one day establish her own support network to help other parents/carers in need and to make everyone feel included.

Living with Autism

Azra Creations Website

Twitter

Instagram

Azra Creations Facebook Page

Contact the author: faria.arsh@gmail.com

Before we begin, I would like to clarify that I will be using the word "child" as a reference to your son or daughter, and they may be in their teens, young adult, or a fully grown adult. This toilet-training program is designed for people with all disabilities and ages, from 3 years of age going up to adulthood.

I will also be using the word "nappy", but some might prefer to use the word "pads", as it seems more appropriate for adults.

Although I talk about autism in this book quite a lot, this program is appropriate for all disabilities and also for some neurotypical children who struggle to grasp the concept of toilet training. Since this is a behavioural method, it can be used for all groups of age and abilities.

There are no right or wrong words here. It's merely my words describing our experience and guiding you to follow steps that will lead to an independent life for your children.

Tips: Keep a marker or sticky notes handy whilst reading this book, so that you can go back to that specific page or paragraph and re-read what you deem is important for your child and you.

I have also left a few blank pages at the back of the book for you to make notes.

Introduction

W hy does any parent want to toilet-train their child? – this is the most important question for toilet training. You need to know your "why". Now, in any other circumstances, the answer is simple. Parents usually start toilet-training routines around the age of 2 years plus, because that's the "norm". Neurotypical children start showing signs of being ready to use the toilet, and this is when most parents get excited about getting rid of nappies and the extra costs that come with it. Toilet training is a difficult task regardless of the ability of the child. I remember that when I toilet-trained my eldest (may I specify she is neurotypical), I found it extremely challenging.

I decided to borrow a book from a friend and read it thoroughly before I embarked on this journey. I cancelled all my plans for a week, had tons of laundry to do each day and, to my surprise, my daughter managed to be fully toilet-trained within a week and a half. To be fair, I started at a later stage of 2 years and 6 months as I wanted to get the job done quickly. I knew that if my daughter was too young, then we wouldn't get anywhere, and it would be frustrating for both of us. After I toilet-trained her, I felt as if I had conquered the world. I know that sounds a little over the top, but ask any parent who has successfully toilet-trained their child—they feel a huge weight off their shoulders.

Now, let's come back to the main topic here. We all hear stories about toilet-training neurotypical children, but is there anyone out there to help us to toilet-train our autistic children or those with additional needs? I remember asking Afiyah's pediatrician, who directed me to the disability nurse. Then we got referred to a continence nurse who gave me a toilet-training leaflet. The information on the leaflet was generic and mainly for neurotypical children – nothing that I hadn't already explored.

Continence nurses are very helpful at dispensing nappies/pads, but for getting our children out of those pads, the answer is hidden in these amazing leaflets that have been doing the rounds for centuries. I don't want to be harsh on any authorities here. They are only doing what they have been told and given by their bosses. Someone is sitting in a posh office with all the facilities and asking their employees to distribute these leaflets to parents in the name of 'support'. My best guess is, none of them know the answer to successful toilet-training strategies for disabled children – or at least in my case, none of them did. After months of chasing authorities and reading more leaflets, I finally bit the bullet and took matters into my own hands.

When it came to getting advice from my friends for Afiyah, I consider myself very lucky as I had the privilege to work as a specialist teaching assistant at an outstanding special school. By the time Afiyah was 9 in 2017, I had gained 6 years of experience at a special school, and I was surrounded by several colleagues who had a wealth of knowledge when it came to autism/disabilities, communication, and behaviour. I had a chat with some of my friends at work who have had previous experience of toilet-training some of their pupils. I also did some internet research and came up with a plan for Afiyah.

With this plan, I felt confident, but at the same time, I was dreading what was to come in the next few weeks. There was excitement and fire in my belly, but also the fear of not achieving our goal. These mixed emotions and feelings don't help us, do they, but as parents (let me add parents of children with additional needs), we are used to dealing with these emotions daily.

With my neurotypical daughter Faiza, I had cleared a week of my schedule, but for Afiyah I had cleared all of 6 weeks of summer holidays. I had a chat with my eldest and explained to her how important this is for Afiyah and her future. Faiza, being the understanding soul she was at that time, (now she's just a grumpy teenager!), she agreed to cooperate as much as possible. Afiyah's dad and I were together at that time, and he was happy for me to get on with the toilet-training program. I did hire some carers to help me, but that stopped in a few weeks because of the inconsistent approach. Any approach for Afiyah must be consistent to enable learning, otherwise, we are just putting pressure on Afiyah and achieving no results.

I know what you all are thinking – why is she going on and on about what happened and when it happened? But trust me, the backstory is as important as the steps that you will read in the next few chapters.

If I am to look back at all the years of Afiyah's life and the struggles we have been through, my heart rate starts rising: From sleepless nights of crying all night (not just Afiyah but me as well), to feeding issues that are also part of autism – which I didn't know at that time, and the whole world blamed me for it, to cleaning up smearing off the walls, carpets, sheets – including more crying all night by me, to now toilet training.

Hand on my heart, I can say that toilet training has been the toughest of them all. Please don't close the book here and lose hope, otherwise this book will be the worst seller, and nobody wants that. I am telling you it's going to be tough, but you will be able to successfully toilet-train your child. You need to know it is tough before you embark on this journey, and this is where I come back to my question of "why" again.

What is your "why" for toilet training your autistic child? Think of this very carefully and hold onto that thought. This thought will give you the strength to carry on this task that no continence nurse or professional has the answer to (yet). This thought will be your driving force to achieve your goal of giving your child the freedom to use the toilet independently.

My "why" with Afiyah was a few reasons. Firstly, Afiyah was diagnosed with recurring UTIs at a young age, and she used to get very ill with it frequently. This resulted in a weakened immune system, more illnesses, and more time off school, and in return, I had to take time off work to look after her. Then Afiyah was prescribed preventative antibiotics that helped to keep these UTIs at bay. One of the main reasons for UTIs (especially in girls) is continence. Antibiotics gave us some relief, but that wasn't the answer, and I couldn't bear the thought of giving those to Afiyah for a long period.

The second reason was quite difficult for me to comprehend, but it was inevitable. With Afiyah being a girl, she will start her menstrual cycle. At that time, even the thought of periods for Afiyah would scare the life out of me. I would think, "As if this poor girl doesn't have enough on her plate as it is, she will have to deal with periods and all that comes with it." I was very keen to get Afiyah out of nappies before she started her periods because if I had left it until later, I would risk confusing Afiyah between sanitary pads and nappies.

Plus, the BIG reason was seeing Afiyah out of nappies and being as independent as she can be to go to the toilet. These three reasons were my driving force to start toilet training.

If your daughter has already started her menstrual cycle, don't worry, and aim to start the program on the last day of her cycle. This will give you full 4 weeks for her to grasp the method, and sanitary pads will not be confused with nappies anymore.

One question I got frequently asked by continence nurses or other professionals is whether Afiyah was showing any signs of being 'ready' for toilet training. Also, if you hear anyone saying, "don't miss the window of opportunity to toilet-train your child", then this is your cue to know they haven't got a clue what they are talking about.

Let me give you all a little glimpse of Afiyah's disability, and you will know if she was ready. Afiyah has severe autism, ADHD, severe learning disability, and epilepsy. She only cares about her food and toys. She can't care less about anything else in the world. Just knowing this is more than enough to conclude that Afiyah could never show signs of being ready for toilet training or ever had a window of opportunity that could be missed.

As far as Afiyah was concerned, nappies were the 'norm' for her, and she didn't know any other way. To be fair to her, why would she know any other way? Going to the toilet will take effort, which means leaving the toys or stopping eating to go to the toilet. Why would Afiyah choose to do that? All parents/carers who have children with autism or other disabilities will know that our children will take the easiest route to do anything.

Let me start again. What I mean to say is all parents will know their children (never mind additional needs) will take the easiest route for everything. Hence, having a nappy on was the best option for Afiyah and sometimes me as well. Imagine if I were out and about in Trafford Centre (something me and the girls loved doing at one point, but not anymore), and Afiyah needed a toilet amid me finding the best bargain of my life. What would be easier for me? Having a nappy on Afiyah, of course. So, obviously, we all got a little too comfortable having nappies on Afiyah as it was the easier option for us for a while. Saying that I knew at the back of my mind that I couldn't let this go on any longer for Afiyah's health and for the other reasons I mentioned earlier.

CHAPTER 1
Autism

The only expert on your child is YOU. I know there are loads of autism and disability experts out there, but they are not the ones living with your child 24/7. No one knows your child inside out as you do, and hence that makes you the expert. I read loads of books on autism when Afiyah was first diagnosed, but what helped me the most was the advice I received from Afiyah's class teachers, TAs, and Speech Therapists, as they are the only people other than me who had hands-on experience of dealing with Afiyah.

The skills that experience gives you, no book, no degree, no profession, can. Hence, it's very important to seek advice from those who have experience in toilet training rather than those who have just read a research paper and given you a leaflet. It's all about putting ideas, theories, and strategies into practice that you and your child's school are doing each day.

Let's go through the triad of impairment once more – I know we all know this by heart now, but this will help us use & implement the strategies for the toilet-training program. There are references at the back of the book for further reading from a research paper, but I have simplified everything in the diagram below.

Social Communication

- Difficulty in using & understanding verbal & non-verbal communication
- Delay in language development
- Limited or no speech
- Echolalia or repeated babbling of the same words
- Absence of facial expressions
- Inability to initiate conversation

Autism Spectrum

Social Interaction

- Inability to handle their own emotions & recognise others' emotions
- Feel distressed if they are required to participate in group activities. They prefer to be alone.
- Rarely develop relationships with others.
- No understanding of others' facial expressions, body language and social cues.

Repetitive behaviour & lack of imagination

- Repetitive behaviour or play patterns
- Inability to imagine situations that are not a part of the daily routine
- Limited set on interests and activities
- Inability to generalise skills learnt in isolation
- Difficulty in thinking in abstract terms.

In this book, we will be touching all three impairments, but repetitive behaviour is the most useful for toilet training. I will be telling you in future chapters how we can use these repetitive behaviours to our & our child's advantage.

When it comes to communication, even the ablest autistic children struggle to communicate their needs in a usual manner. To be fair to them, how many of us know how to communicate our needs properly – this is one of my favourite topics, but I am not going to dive into this now. Afiyah uses PECS to communicate her needs regarding food and to ask to go to the toilet. When Afiyah and I were introduced to PECS, I was fascinated by this approach. I knew I had to tap into it at home so that we could inculcate good communication habits in Afiyah. In one of the PECS training sessions, I was told that Afiyah should make 40 PECS requests at home, and what do I do? I started counting the number of requests Afiyah was making. Please don't laugh at me. I promise I am not a nerd (not that there is anything wrong with being a nerd), but I am just trying to paint a picture of my enthusiasm for PECS and Afiyah's communication. This definitely came in handy when I started toilet-training Afiyah.

But what if your child does not use PECS and is verbal – I was asked this question in one of the toilet-training workshops I once held alongside an amazing colleague/class teacher who is now doing an amazing job helping other families. My answer is, even if your child has never used PECS and is completely verbal, I would still introduce a 'toilet' symbol only for toilet-training purposes. As we all know, autistic children are visual learners – despite their comprehension, understanding, and verbal communication, a visual symbol makes more sense, and they are more likely to comprehend and retain that information for longer. Remember, it's not just about understanding but also about retaining the information that visual symbols will help our children do.

So far, we have touched on 'communication' from the triad of impairments. I will talk about more strategies in the next few chapters that will help your child to retain information, which will fall under another topic.

Social interaction will also play a big role (not a major one, though) when it comes to toilet training. Our children will best learn new skills from people they trust. We can't expect a new community nurse to join the class team and start toilet-training strategies on the first day. Anyone who is toilet training your child should have some sort of bond with them – hence the best person is you (parents/carers), a childminder whom your child knows, their class teacher/ TAs, etc. You get the picture. If you are employing someone specially to help you with toilet training, it's best for them to start a few days in advance to form a bond with your child. This will enable your child to trust them.

Now let's come to the most important triad of impairment that we will use to our advantage in this process – repetitive behaviour. Generally, Afiyah's repetitive behaviours get on my nerves. I know it's part of Afiyah, but it can be very inconvenient at times. Keeping up with the exact routine of how she wants to do things is difficult, and if things don't happen in the same order, we get a major tantrum and a lot of behaviour. I have put in loads of strategies at home to deal with her rigid and repetitive behaviours, but I won't be talking about those strategies in this book at all. In fact, I will use those rigid behaviours to help us toilet-train our children. Since we know that our autistic children thrive on routine, we are going to gently introduce toilet training strategies as part of their routine, and this is how we are going to achieve our goal.

I'll go back to the paragraph where I mentioned professionals asking me whether Afiyah was showing any signs of being toilet-trained – my answer was no. If your child is showing signs, that's great, but the type of toilet training strategy I will be showing you is 'behavioural training'. This can be done regardless of the abilities of your child, their age, or their difficulties. Let me specify that your child should be mobile to be behaviorally trained to use the toilet – this is the minimum requirement we are going to need to start. We want to make going to the toilet a habit, so basically, we are teaching your child a new habit/new behaviour.

Since our children thrive on routine, we can use this to our advantage. Make going to the toilet part of their routine in a very structured way for a long period so that it becomes their habit. I had done some research about how long it takes to form a new habit. Research done by Phillippa Lally, a health psychology researcher at University College London, found that, on average, it takes over 2 months before a new behaviour becomes automatic – 66 days, to be exact. This was published in the *European Journal of Social Psychology*. There are references given at the end of the book. Please check them out and do further reading if you wish to.

Please don't panic about the figure of 66 days given in this research. Let me remind you that this research was done on neurotypical people, and for autistic children, picking up a new routine takes a lot less time than that. This is why I keep saying we will use their repetitive behaviour to our advantage. Plus, we are going to make this 'new routine' so enticing that they will want to do it and won't be thrown by it. Hopefully, it will be a win-win for all of us.

As I mentioned earlier in the book, I had to clear 6 weeks of our schedule to toilet train Afiyah. This may not apply to everyone. What you must know is that I was adapting and learning as I went along, but now, I have a toilet-training program at hand that will help other children and families. Also, Afiyah has profound needs, which many of your children might have, but for those who don't have such profound learning difficulties like Afiyah, you can easily expect your child to be trained in a shorter time frame.

CHAPTER 2

When?

N ow you know your 'why', it's time to think about 'when' you can embark on this journey.

As you have read in the previous chapters, I toilet-trained Afiyah during the summer break. I feel this is the best time as you have long enough to work on this program and you are under less pressure from a time point of view. You can choose other school breaks, like Easter break, but because it only gives you a couple of weeks, you will be putting a lot of pressure on yourself and your child too. I know summer break is the busiest time for us, but since the weather is nice, your child can be in the garden, and if there are any accidents (which there will be), it'll be easier to clean. For all the reasons mentioned above, summer break might be your best bet.

When you have a specific time blocked for this program, you can plan ahead. You can plan to hire specific support to help you toilet-train, you can prepare meals in advance and freeze them for later, or you can ask your family and friends to help with your other children, and so on.

Remember one thing: you are as important as your children. You need to make sure you are prepared for this – I'm not trying to scare you when I say 'prepared for this', but what I mean is I want you to be prepared with tools for your success.

For years, everyone told me it was all about Afiyah and it wasn't about me, and, to be honest, I believed it, and I started saying that to myself too. The truth is, it's about Afiyah, and it's also about me as her primary carer. We both go hand in hand. If I am well, I can look after Afiyah properly, and then Afiyah can thrive in her life. When I feel well supported by others, I can support Afiyah better. Hence, I want you to remember that you are as important as your child/child's needs in this process and throughout your life.

Let's go back to being 'prepared'. Make sure you have enough support from your partner or your family & friends. In my case, I just needed my husband (ex now) to be on the same page. When I say the same page, I mean in agreement that he is happy for me to get on with toilet training and that he will entertain my other daughter during the summer break.

Support comes in many forms; it doesn't mean physical help with toilet training, but also as moral support. I can't emphasise enough how much moral support can help a family in need. So, think carefully about who can be supportive in whatever form possible. Talk to those people, let them know what kind of help/support you may need during the summer break, and act on it. It is very important to know that asking for help doesn't make you weak. In fact, it's the opposite. Seeking any form of help shows your strength and determination to achieve your goals for your children.

CHAPTER 3
Preparation

I f you have a good understanding of the first 2 chapters, then this will be an easy one to understand. I'm going to keep everything extremely simple and easy to follow. All you must do is follow the steps exactly. I know all our children are unique in terms of their specific needs, but this is a behavioural training method. This training is very specific and will work for all abilities and ages.

Let's face it, when it comes to behaviour, we are talking about human behaviour, and this has been researched for years. Despite being from different backgrounds, we humans have very similar behaviours. Now, let's narrow that down to autistic behaviour. Despite having different behavioural challenges, the core of behaviour and its analysis remains the same. Hence, I need you to follow this program in a very specific way, otherwise you may not see the results you want, and you could end up in a vicious cycle of not grasping the method.

1. Find 2 motivators – this could be a toy, your child's tablet, a video game, or a food item. Do yourself a favour, and don't choose items that you/your child cannot live without. For example, if your child is used to playing on the iPad as soon as they wake up, then don't choose iPad as a motivator. I want

you to think of items that are a great incentive and can only be given as a reward for toilet-training purposes only.

2. Motivator No. 1 – this is for when your child is sitting on the toilet. Our children have never sat on the toilet, so they are not used to sitting on it. Why would they be used to it? They have never had to. They have always had the luxury of having a wee and poo in their nappies whenever and wherever they want to. So, they will need a motivator to be sat on the toilet. For Afiyah, I had kept a small basket of toys on the toilet windowsill, and she only had access to these toys when she was sitting on the toilet. I had a few toothbrushes (anyone who knows Afiyah will know how much she loves toothbrushes), a few cause-and-effect toys, and a few sensory toys. I had removed all the cause-and-effect toys, sensory toys, and toothbrushes from the toy boxes around the house, and only limited those for her to access whilst she was sitting on the toilet. She still had access to toys, but the best ones were in the toilet for her to play with whilst she was sitting on the toilet. I am sure you get the gist here, and, by now, you have the perfect motivators in your mind for this purpose and this purpose only. If you have multiple bathrooms, make sure you have the same basket and similar toys in all your toilets. We want to keep everything consistent here to avoid any confusion and to make this process easy and simple for you and your child. I bought a bunch of things from Poundland to avoid expensive toys.

3. Motivator No. 2 – this is going to be the ultimate motivator for your child. Think about something your child can only have when they have successfully used the toilet to have a wee or poo. If you knew Afiyah, you would have guessed it by now and said 'food'. Yes, Afiyah is a big foodie, and she has a sweet tooth, just like her mum. It was a no-brainer for me that it was going to be a sweet food item for Afiyah. I bought a small box of Haribos and left it on the windowsill in the toilet. Sometimes this would trigger Afiyah's behaviour because when she saw the box, she wanted sweets instantly without having a successful wee in the toilet. During these times, I used to hide the box on the porch, which was luckily just next to the toilet. Long story short, be prepared to hide this motivator from their vision temporarily to avoid any behavioural triggers. Since I was using a sweet food item as a motivator for Afiyah, I eliminated all the other puddings and sweets from her diet all day long. This meant Afiyah did not have access to sweet items at any time other than when she had had a successful wee or a poo into the toilet. Can you now see how enticing it was for her to successfully hold her wee and only release her bladder into the toilet so that she could get her sweets as a reward? I am sure you have grasped the concept of both motivators now.

4. You need a timer. I don't want you to use the timer on your phone, as that will confuse your child. I would like you to use a specific timer for toilet training only. This will make your child associate this specific timer with toilet-training purposes.

Your child is definitely going to learn quicker and better by you buying a separate timer. I bought ours online, which cost me £4.50. I bought a couple just in case I lose one. It's always best to be prepared with a backup plan for the things we can control. I've said this before, and I'll say this again – you are very important in this process, and I am keeping your well-being at the centre of this as well as your child's. I want you to have all the tools at hand so that you feel prepared and confident.

5. You know that sitting on a higher chair with our feet unable to touch the ground makes us feel uncomfortable, and we are more likely to lose our balance. This applies to our children sitting on the toilet. When they are sat on the toilet, we need to make sure they feel safe and protected. The last thing we want is for our children to develop a fear of the toilet. To make sure our children feel safe, you will need a step that you can place under your child's feet. This will not only make them feel safe and comfortable, but it is also essential to have a bowel movement. Having their feet firmly against something gives them the right posture and position that helps with a bowel movement. If your toilet seats are very wide for your child, you will also need a seat insert so that your child can sit comfortably. Afiyah was already 9 years old, and I didn't need an insert. Everything these days is on the click of our fingers and look at these items as an investment into your child's independent future.

6. I have included visual symbols that you will need. Please scan the barcode for paper copies or click on the link if you are reading an e-book. You will find these at the end of this chapter. You can print these symbols and laminate them, or you can send a copy to your child's school to print and laminate for you. I am sure your child's school will be happy to help. I will talk through each visual symbol so that you know exactly how and when to use them. The 'toilet' symbol is pretty self-explanatory. I want you to go around your house and stick this symbol in different areas of your house. Think of the areas your child hangs around most. Definitely have 1 symbol outside the toilet door. Again, if you have multiple toilets in your house, make sure you have 1 'toilet' symbol outside each toilet. If your child has a PECS book, put one symbol on the top of the book as well. If your child spends most of the time in the garden, then have a symbol board outside with them. If your child likes to be in the lounge, then have the symbol handy somewhere in the lounge. The 'go' symbol needs to stay in the toilet. This is for a very specific purpose that I'll explain more in-depth later in the book. I would ask you to use velcro or blue tac to stick the 'go' symbol on one of the walls inside the toilet. I am sorry that I am not very considerate of your home décor here, and I am asking you to stick symbols on your walls which might leave marks. So, please think carefully and stick these symbols where the vanity of your beautiful home is not being compromised. I have given up on what my house looks like anymore. Afiyah has

worked hard to destroy every part of my house, and hence I am

not fussed about sticking several symbols all around my house.

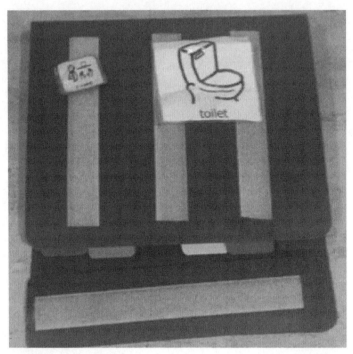

7. Fluids – raise your hand if you drink enough fluids per day. Never mind our kids; my water intake is terrible. One of the main reasons is I don't feel thirsty enough to remember to have a drink of water at regular intervals throughout the day. I am guilty of not giving Afiyah enough fluids in the past, but we have luckily changed our habits over time. Afiyah is very good at using her PECS book to ask for all sorts of foods, but she will never ask for water. I don't think she knows what thirst feels like. I remember Afiyah hardly having any water throughout the day. She would have a bit of orange juice after her meals, but that was it. It surely wasn't healthy. I remember buying different beakers, hoping that Afiyah would start drinking water or ever cordial through those, but I was unsuccessful. So, when it came to toilet training, I soon realised that fluid intake was the key. Imagine you have had more water than usual; you are more like to feel a fuller bladder than normal, and you will have the urge to wee more often. We are trying to induce the feeling of a 'fuller' bladder with our children. We know what that feeling is, but our children might not know, as they probably never had enough water in a day to have a full bladder.

Or, even if our children know the feeling of a full bladder, they don't know to release bladder control only into the toilet. Through this toilet-training program, you will be teaching your child the art of bladder control. In Afiyah's case, I can certainly

27

say she had never had enough fluids at a time per day to have a full bladder. So, when it came to toilet training, all I had to do was buy a fruit shoot bottle, empty it, pour cordial in it (I made a strong one as I knew Afiyah would like it), and give her a few sips every 15 minutes. Yes, you read that right – every 15 minutes. I told you it's not easy, but it certainly is possible. Because I had put everything aside and dedicated all my time and energy to this task, giving Afiyah a few sips of drink every 15 minutes didn't seem too much of an issue for me. If your child is good at drinking fluids throughout the day then increase their fluid intake a little bit. Instead of a few sips every 15 minutes, you can give a quarter or half a cup every half hour. Our aim here is to offer more fluids than their usual intake to induce the feeling of a full bladder. I found it easier to maintain a water diary every day for this.

At that time, I was writing on a random piece of paper, but if I had my time again, I would maintain a proper water diary. This way, I could keep track of how much water Afiyah was having per day and, more importantly, I could understand how her body worked. For example, if I had given her a few sips of drink at 11 a.m. and she ended up having a wee accident at 11:20 a.m., keeping a diary of fluid intake gave me a rough idea that her bladder was able to hold these fluids for less than 20 minutes, and then I could use this information to my advantage. I'll be talking more about fluids in the next chapter. For now, all you need to know is that you need to find a way to get a few sips. Yes, only a few sips of fluids into your child's system every 15 minutes will do the trick, and that'll be the best start yet.

Here's the list of things you need:

1. Motivator No. 1 and No. 2

2. Timer.

3. Step – depending on your child's height.

4. Toilet seat insert, depending on your child's size.

5. Fluids.

6. Visual symbols of 'toilet' and 'go' hand – included with the purchase of this book.

7. Toilet training data sheet and drink tracker – both included with the purchase of this book.

Barcode for 'toilet' symbol

Barcode for 'go' symbol

Barcode for toilet-training data-sheet PDF

Barcode for drink tracker PDF

Above is everything you need to be ready to start toilet training. So here we go...

STEP 4

How?

Hang on a second. This chapter says, 'Step 4'. Where are the first few steps?

W‌ell, if you have jumped to this chapter in the hope of going to the program straight away, then I'm afraid it's not a good idea. Go back and read the introduction as well as the first 3 chapters, because they are as important as this one.

We have touched on 'why' and 'when', and we have also gone through the checklist of things you need to be fully prepared. Now it's time to talk about 'how'.

"Yes, yes, yes… the moment I've been waiting for!", I hear you say.

This is the step-by-step guide I need you to follow exactly.

Day 1

1. Timer – after your child's morning routine, remove their nappy, give them a few sips of drink, and set the timer to go off in 15 minutes.

2. The timer goes off – let's just say your child is watching tele, playing on their iPad, or playing in the garden. Doesn't matter where your child is. I want you to take the timer near your child whilst it's still beeping so that your child can hear it, and take

31

the 'toilet' symbol in your hand. Let's say the 'toilet' symbol is in your right hand. Use your left hand to guide your child to point and touch the 'toilet' symbol. Then gently hold your child's hand and take them to the toilet. I want you to keep your language to a minimum. Don't overstimulate your child with loads of words, sentences, etc... Just use keywords. Say "toilet" when you get them to point to the 'toilet' symbol, and only use hand gestures to get them to move and go to the toilet. You may want to hold their hand and take them to the toilet with you.

3. When they are in the toilet – depending on your child's abilities, they might take their trousers & pants off by themselves, or you may need to help them. I would like to emphasise one thing, though. I don't want you to use this opportunity to try to teach them other new skills of undressing or dressing. Our focus here is to get our children to use the toilet independently. Trying to teach them dressing and undressing skills whilst toilet training will lead to a lot of confusion and frustration for both of you. I want you to take that pressure off yourself and your child and only focus on one skill at a time. If your child already knows how to take their trousers/pants off and sit on the toilet, all well and good, but if they don't, I want you to help them undress their bottom half of clothing and gently guide them to sit on the toilet seat.

4. It is very important that boys also sit on the toilet, even for a wee. I know you might want to get them used to having a wee

whilst stood up so they can use a urinal in the future, but at this time, we follow a blanket rule for all, and that is sitting on the toilet.

5. Once they are sat on the toilet, bring the basket of motivators that you have already prepared. Give them this option, and let's hope they find the toy they like and keep busy with it for a few minutes.

6. Being seated on the toilet – this is not as easy and simple as we think it might be. For toilet-training purposes, any child should be sat on the toilet for at least 2 minutes at a time for their body to realise and work to release bladder control or to have a bowel movement. If they can sit for longer, that's great, but you don't want them to be sat for a long time and develop a dislike of the toilet, especially since we are trying to make it extremely enticing. Here, use your timer again. I want you to set the timer for 30 seconds – I am starting with 30 seconds, keeping in mind your child is not used to being sat on the toilet at all. Once you have set the timer for 30 seconds and it goes off, I want you to take the 'go' hand symbol in your hand, and get your child to tap on the 'go' hand. Whilst they tap on the 'go' hand, you need to say, "you can go", and gently guide them to get off the toilet seat. Whilst they are getting off the toilet seat, praise them with simple keywords. Use these words only "Good sitting on the toilet", and "Good girl/good boy".

Gently place the basket in front of them and get them to leave those toys in the basket so you can leave it on the windowsill for their next visit. They may not want to let go of those toys, but gently encourage them to put the toys into the basket. Having a visual basket to leave toys behind is a good way of giving a non-verbal prompt without getting into a fight/argument with them. Let's be honest, our kids love a good fight over anything and everything. That's our life day in and out.

You must be thinking that I have asked to get your child to sit on the toilet for 2 minutes, and I've just contradicted myself by setting the timer for 30 seconds. Here, I am trying to get your child into a habit of sitting on the toilet without causing them any distress or dislike of toilets. It's very important to gradually build everything and be extremely gentle in our approach to make sure it's a positive experience for your child and you. This way, you will have less behavioural backlash and less stress for you, your child, and your whole family. Saying that, be prepared for some backlash and behaviour, and I am sure you are extremely skilled in dealing with these behaviours by now and know how to work around them in order to get your child to comply with the demands placed on them. Slowly build the length of time your child is able to sit on the toilet at once. So, next time your child is sitting on the toilet, set the timer for 32 seconds, and then, as soon as it goes off, use the 'go' hand symbol to give them a cue to stand up and leave the toilet. Follow this gradual process to increase the time your child is able to sit on the toilet seat each time until they reach the target of 2 minutes. The 2-second increase in time can be done every time on the same day, or you can go slower and increase 2 seconds only once a day. The point I'm trying to make is you know your child best, and your aim here is to make sure your child isn't getting distressed by sitting on the toilet. So, judge the situation accordingly and increase time depending on your child's abilities or mood.

7. On day 1, you are setting the timer to 15 minutes throughout the day. You are also giving your child a few sips of water/drink every 15 minutes. To make tracking all of this easy, I have included toileting charts and a drink tracker with this book. Remember the rules of simple language, keywords, timer, go hand, etc. Now, I'll tell you what you need to do when they have a wee or poo accident, and also what to do when they have had a successful wee/poo or both into the toilet.

8. Accidents/not being able to wee/poo or both into the toilet – this is one of the most important notes I want you to read, remember, and engrave in your minds. I can't emphasise enough how important this is because this will determine how quickly your child learns to go to the toilet independently. When they have had an accident in their pants, DO NOT, and I repeat, DO NOT under any circumstances give them any verbal reaction. DO NOT give them any eye contact. DO NOT utter a

single word out of your mouth. DO NOT say anything to your child. Just very casually get them cleaned and changed into new clothing.

Remember, accidents are going to happen. They have never used the toilet before, and this will happen several times a day. Be prepared with loads of clothing at hand, towels, tissues, cleaning material, or whatever you need to clean your child and mess with no commotion. Again, I will emphasise that all the above is imperative to avoid negativity of any form for your child and you. The reason behind this is that, as humans, we are more likely to pick up on negative cues and behaviours first than positive ones. Our children with autism or any additional needs tend to respond more to negative behaviours compared to positive ones. Hence, we are completely avoiding any scenarios where there might be a possibility of picking up negative behaviours at all. After you have changed your child, set the timer to 15 mins, and see how it goes. If your child is having a wee before the 15-minute timer goes off, then try reducing the time to 10 minutes. try to find a pattern and look for cues where you can and use that to your advantage.

9. What to do when they have had a successful wee/poo or both into the toilet – this is our dream come true. This is what we want each time and every day for the rest of our life. So, we treat this like it's the best thing ever. This is the time to bring out your ultimate motivator. Remember I told you about 2

motivators: one for sitting on the toilet and one for when they have been successful. This is the time to use our most important motivator No. 2. For Afiyah, it was sweets/Haribos. Break sweets into smaller pieces if you are concerned about their teeth or eating habits, but only give them this specific sweet/treat after having a successful wee/poo into the toilet. Let's imagine your child has had a successful wee into the toilet. At that moment, I want you to quickly bring out the sweet/food item/whatever motivator you have chosen and give it to them instantly whilst saying: "{your child's name}, had a wee on the toilet, well done {child's name}".

Let them enjoy their motivator, feel appreciated for having a wee, and then after you know they have finished, use your 'go' hand to give them a cue to get up and leave the toilet. Regarding cleaning them with tissues, I would rather you not emphasise on teaching them this skill yet. I would rather you use toilet roll to clean them, help them put their pants and trousers back on, help them wash their hands, and leave the toilet on a happy note. Don't bother teaching them to flush the toilet unless they really love doing that out of their will. Our focus is and should always remain on getting them to use the toilet positively and giving them praise + their motivators for successfully having a wee and poo into the toilet. After 6 years of successful toileting for Afiyah, because of her profound needs, I have to clean her after her bowel movements. She can clean herself after emptying her bladder, but that's the best I can get out of her, and it's okay. She is my daughter, and if I have to carry on cleaning her on the toilet, I don't mind. What I did start to be uncomfortable with was changing her nappies. Maybe 'uncomfortable' isn't the right word, but she is a big girl, and if I were still changing her nappies, I would have found it physically challenging.

10. It's time for bed now. You are exhausted, and so is your child, as they are learning something completely new. It's time to put their nappies back on for the night. At this moment, we are only concentrating on the daytime routine, and trust me, having a nappy on at night WILL NOT confuse your child. Afiyah was fully toilet-trained within 6 weeks, but she stayed in nappies at night for months after. I know many children who stay in nappies at night for longer than you would want to, and that's okay. Eventually, we reached a stage when Afiyah started having dry nappies every morning consistently, and that's when I knew she was ready for the nappy to come off at night as well. Remember I emphasised tracking their fluids. This plays a huge role in getting rid of nappies at night. I would stop all fluids 1 hour prior to bedtime and then make sure I use the timer to get Afiyah to the toilet before I settle her into her bed. This meant Afiyah had emptied her bladder before bed and most likely won't need a wee in the middle of the night.

By the end of this toilet-training program, you will be the ultimate expert on what to do and when to do it. I am sure you will know when it's time to get rid of nappies at nighttime.

Day 2

1. Regardless of how many accidents we have had on day 1, we are starting day 2 on a positive note. We want to keep everything positive for our children and us. After your child's morning routine, it's time for their nappy to come off again.

2. Set the timer to 15 minutes again, give a few sips of water/drink every 15 minutes, keep track of water intake, keep track of accidents, successful wees/poos, etc... Keeping track is the key as this will give you an idea of your child's pattern. You can look back at the charts at the end of the day and admire your hard work and your child's success. I still have Afiyah's toileting charts that I bring out from time to time to remind myself of her and my achievements. Yes, it's your achievement, too. Remember that you are as important as your child is in this whole process. Never underestimate your achievements, and never let anyone tell you otherwise. I may be sounding really American here (nothing against being American or sounding like one), but we Brits have a habit of beating ourselves up for no reason. Hence, let's be a little American and praise ourselves, and give ourselves the importance and respect we deserve as parents & carers. (Sorry for digressing, but empowerment is very important).

Let me go through the steps very quickly once more. Set the timer for 15 mins, and give plenty of fluids (whilst keeping track). When accidents happen, don't respond, no eye contact or verbal response, and just clean without commotion. Obviously, the accidents are happening before the timer has gone off, which means that straight after the accidents, you restart the timer and set it for 15 minutes. The timer goes off, and your child needs to hear the timer. You take the 'toilet' symbol with you to the child, and gently guide them to touch the toilet symbol whilst you say the word "toilet". You then gently guide them into the toilet, help them to undress, and sit on the toilet seat. Get them to sit for 2 minutes at once but build it up slowly with 30 seconds at first. Give them the first set of motivators whilst they are sat on the toilet. As soon as the timer goes off after 30 seconds (or more), use the 'go' hand as a cue, get them to tap the symbol whilst you say, "you can go", and let them get up and leave the toilet. Let's hope whilst they were sitting on the toilet, they happened to have a wee or a poo, and at that moment, you will praise them by saying "{child name} had a wee/poo", "well done {child's name}" and whilst you are praising, you give them the sweet/motivator No. 2 at the same time. By doing this, you are creating a link of reward system between them having a wee/poo into the toilet and you giving them a reward at that very moment. The rewards need to be instant for them to grasp the concept of what they are getting it for. Remember to keep your verbal language to a minimum, only use keywords.

Day 3

New day, and it's a positive day despite the number of accidents the day before. I know exactly the emotions you will be going through after every accident, but don't give up hope, and don't beat yourself. It's never your fault, and you already know that it's not your child's fault, either. Just tell yourself that it's a gradual process and it will take time.

If there have been fewer accidents on day 2 compared to day 1, then increase the timer to 20 mins on day 3, but if you find that 20 minutes is too long of a gap, then reduce the time back to 15 minutes. I know what you are thinking now: you are wondering if your life will be about 15-20-minute timers forever, but let me give you good news. It won't be, at least it won't be for long. You will make progress; it may just be an extra 1 minute each day, and that's how you will eventually reach a reasonable time of 1-hour gaps between timers. Your child will also reach a stage when they won't need a timer at all.

You are to increase 5 minutes or less each day depending on the ratios of wees/poos into the toilet to accidents; in favour of more wees/poos into the toilet.

This is how you will carry on each day. Always remember the dos and don'ts that are crucial in every part of this process. My advice at this point is not to jump straight to toilet training without reading further chapters. You have only just begun, and there is so much more for you to learn before you start teaching your child. By the end of this book, you will be fully prepared to embark on this journey, and I hope you won't look back.

CHAPTER 5

Timer

The timer – why is the timer so important here? The timer is our lifesaver. The timer means we are not giving any verbal prompts and making our children dependent on us having to tell them every time. The timer is merely an auditory cue, and your child will pick up very quickly that: when this noise goes off, I go to the toilet, when I sit on the toilet, I get my motivators to sit on the toilet, and when I have a wee into the toilet, I get my ultimate reward with positive praise and love from my parents/carers.

Before toilet-training programs, I used to be heavily involved with the speech and language team to help parents implement communication methods at home. With every communication method, whether it be PECS, talking tools, or other methods, all speech and language therapists teach us NOT to use any verbal prompts. The idea here is to make our children communicate independently and positively in whatever form they can. For example, a non-verbal child should NOT be given any verbal prompts to use their PECS book. Instead, they are supposed to be given a non-verbal/hand-over-hand approach to access their PECS book to choose the right symbol they want.

If I were to start giving verbal prompts such as "Afiyah, go to your PECS book and show me what you want", or I were to point at her book and say, "Afiyah, show me", then Afiyah will always wait for me to give her verbal prompts/instructions to choose a symbol from her PECS book.

(If you have skipped the above paragraph, thinking this may not apply to your child because they don't use PECS, then I'm afraid you are wrong. I really need you to read the above paragraph to understand the importance of non-verbal prompts).

Now, let's apply the above strategy for toilet-training purposes. If I want Afiyah to go to the toilet by herself without me reminding her every time, and let's face it, I can't be physically there to remind her, then I really need to apply the non-verbal strategy to this process. This is where I say the timer is our lifesaver. By using the timer, I am eliminating any verbal prompts – basically, I am not saying "Afiyah, go to the toilet now", etc. When the timer goes off, Afiyah hears the sound and takes that as a cue to go to the toilet.

So, once again, let's go through the steps of how to use the timer. The timer goes off, you take the timer near your child, the child has heard the timer, you have the 'toilet' symbol in one hand, and you use the other hand to gently guide your child to tap the symbol, you say the word "toilet" whilst they tap the symbol, then you gently guide your child to go to the toilet. During this time, you DON'T use any verbal prompts and DON'T use any verbal language other than the word 'toilet' when your child taps the symbol. By using this non-verbal approach, you have eliminated all verbal prompts and any chances of your child being prompt-dependent. The idea here is to make your child independent to go to the toilet and, most importantly, make life easier for you and give you a bit of peace of mind.

When I practiced this method, within the first few days, Afiyah had grasped the concept of a timer, and the minute she heard the timer go off, she automatically got up from whatever she was doing and ran to the toilet. This is what I was saying in earlier chapters. This is how we are going to use our children's repetitive behaviour to our advantage. Our kids thrive on routine, and the timer going off is now part of their new routine, and they will recognise that sound and take themselves to the toilet. This is the first major step you have achieved, and this was only possible because you have NOT used any verbal prompts. I am sure you now understand the importance of non-verbal cues in this process.

As time goes on and you are following all the steps of using the timer, motivator No. 1, 'go' hand symbol, and motivator No. 2, your child will start making sense of the whole process. It's almost like connecting dots in their mind, and you are helping them to connect these dots by delivering a very well-planned and managed behavioural strategy.

We are using repetitive, rigid, and specific strategies to create new positive behaviour for our children. Can you see how powerful this method is and how much you can achieve when you follow the steps exactly and precisely mentioned in this book?

Soon you will start seeing that your child understands they get this lovely reward (motivator No. 2) and lovely praise when they have a wee/poo into the toilet. This will then encourage your child to hold their wee or wait for the timer to go off. Most of the time, they will just get up and take themselves to the toilet or might give you the symbol of the toilet or might say the word "toilet" if they need a toilet before the timer goes off. All of these are perfectly fine because your child has initiated it. If your child takes themselves to the toilet without saying anything, follow them and reward them after having a wee/poo. If they give you the toilet symbol, just say the word "toilet" and take them, and if they say the word "toilet", guide them into the toilet without saying anything. After all the above, reward them with their motivator No. 2, as mentioned before. Always remember to reward because that is the reinforcement that makes your child go to the toilet.

Just like that, your child has taken themselves to the toilet, and this is the happiest moment of your life – well, this was one of the happiest moments of my life without any exaggeration.

When things start moving in a positive direction each day, and you are seeing fewer accidents, don't suddenly stop using the timer or start giving them verbal prompts to go. Use the timer for at least 3 months before you start thinking of stopping it. You will know when your child is completely independent and going to the toilet without a timer. As I said earlier in this book, you are the best expert when it comes to your child and trust your instincts.

CHAPTER 6

Bowel Movements

I cannot believe I have named a chapter in my book after 'Bowel Movements'. What has my life come to??!!!!

Saying that, when you have a child with autism or other additional needs, we all have way too many poo stories to share. From when they realised they could have sensory play with their own poo in the middle of the night to when they accidentally ate it. I must say I used to find both quite disturbing. It is no secret that autistic children have huge sensory impairments, and this often leads to smearing. I remember the times when Afiyah used to smear her faeces all over her room in the middle of the night, and I used to find her in the horror of being covered in it. I can never forget that sight, and I am sure each parent who has seen that is a little scarred for life.

The hours of cleaning her in the bath, then cleaning her room and sanitising everything was only a small part, but the fact that my daughter had so little understanding that she was covered in her own poo was the ultimate soul crusher. The debilitating thoughts of what her future will be and the heightened emotions of whether she will ever learn and what if she can't were beyond anything I had experienced.

I don't think the world out there has even 1% of understanding of what we parents and carers go through every single day. I don't know how we do it and how we have come so far, but I do know the only driving force is the love for our children. This is the only explanation I have when I think of everything we have been through.

There are many positives to toilet training, and one of them is the fact that there are fewer opportunities to smear. With any child being able to poo into the toilet, they simply don't have the means and access to be able to smear anymore.

Afiyah has always had constipation since she was 2 years old. After trying changes in her diet, which she was very resistant to and going to several GPs and pediatricians, she was finally prescribed Lactulose and Senakot. I wish they had given these laxatives to Afiyah earlier and prevented a lot of pain and suffering, but we sadly live in a world where professionals don't believe us parents and tell us the magic solution of a healthier diet.

We all know a healthy diet will help bowel movements, but most of our autistic children don't like to eat the things that are going to help them have bowel movements easily. I have implemented some healthy eating habits recently because we are at a stage where we can work on that, but I won't be asking you to do any of that. Just carry on with whatever foods your child is already eating because our focus at this moment in time is toilet training.

I would definitely advise you to seek medical advice if your child is constipated. Being constipated is horrible. It can leave our children with the trauma of avoiding the urge to have a bowel movement, and then they get into a vicious cycle of holding their poo, which makes them more constipated. So, if your child is suffering from constipation, please speak with your GP; they may be able to prescribe something that will ease constipation and pain.

I can say from my experience that Senakot was a good one for Afiyah. Afiyah was on Lactulose and Senakot to start off with, but then we got to a stage when she was only on Senakot. I liked Senakot for a few reasons. First, it's derived from senna leaves, and second, Senakot is known to create muscle movement in the digestive system, leading to a bowel movement. So, every time Afiyah was about to have a bowel movement in her nappy, she would groan, indicating she was about to have a poo.

When it came to toilet training, I was able to use this to my advantage. Every time Afiyah made a groaning sound, and she also had a habit of holding the end of the settee whilst standing in a corner, this was a cue for me to rush her to the toilet. This helped me tremendously to know when she was about to have a bowel movement, and I was able to act quickly on it and take her to the toilet in time. Sometimes we wouldn't make it in time, but that was okay. Sometimes Afiyah had a little poo in her pants and the rest into the toilet. I would still reward Afiyah for having some poo into the toilet as I wanted her to understand the concept of reward for a poo into the toilet – this sounds so weird, but I'm going to roll with it (not roll in it, don't get that idea, I know exactly how your mind works!).

So, Afiyah understood the sensation of bowel movements before she learned bladder control. By me picking up on her cues, then taking her to the

49

toilet quickly, and then rewarding her for having a poo into the toilet, she grasped the concept of opening her bowels into the toilet quicker than I imagined.

If your child is already displaying some specific cues and has habits to do with having a wee or poo into their nappy, start making a note of it. This will come in handy when you get rid of their nappy and start this program.

If I were to understand things from Afiyah's point of view and how she understands her body, she is more likely to feel the urge for bowel movements first compared to having a full bladder and learning bladder control. This does not mean your child will do exactly the same. Some children understand bladder control better than bowel movements. Most of the time, when I see problems with learning to open bowels into the toilet, it's mainly related to an underlying primary reason, and constipation is one of them.

Hence, I would like to emphasise that if your child has an existing underlying condition related to bowel movements, please get that checked first, and then only you can start toilet training. I wouldn't advise starting this process without having all the answers and solutions to existing medical conditions that will have an impact on their learning.

As humans, our bodies work in similar ways. Hence, most of us feel the urge to have a bowel movement after a meal. Now, we may have adapted this urge over time due to our lifestyle or work commitments, as, let's be honest, most of us don't fancy having a poo at work after our lunch. However, I don't understand why that's such a huge deal. I think it's healthy to have a poo when we need to. Maybe I'll write another book on how to have a poo at work. Look out for this one in the next few years!

Jokes apart, your child is most likely to have a bowel movement 15-30 minutes after having a meal. Now, this information gives you an edge. It gives you a chance to be prepared for a bowel movement and perhaps set the timer accordingly. I would go one step further and ask you to time how long it takes your child to open their bowels from when they finish their meal. You can do this little exercise whilst they are still in nappies, and if your child's body is consistent with a specific time window for a bowel movement, then bingo, you are out to a great start already.

Disclaimer – I have mentioned the medicines Afiyah has had in the past, but this is not an indication for you to start your child on any medication without consulting your medical practitioner. Some medicines might interact with others, and some might start an allergic reaction. Hence, please DO NOT under any circumstances start any medicines without consulting your child's GP, pediatrician, or any other medical practitioner your child is seeing.

CHAPTER 7

No Verbal Prompts

and

What to do When There are Setbacks

O ne thing that you must do at all times is NO VERBAL PROMPTS. This should be your mantra from the start until your child is with you. After all these years, I still don't give Afiyah any verbal prompts, and, in the past, she has had a few blips because someone in her primary school might have given verbal prompts a few times. Just a few verbal prompts were enough to set her back, and she started having wee accidents again.

Whoever had done this was obviously not doing it on purpose. It was a genuine and simple mistake but had major consequences. I felt all my hard work and Afiyah's achievements were lost. Luckily, I was wrong because I quickly fell back to the basics and revisited all the initial strategies, which meant Afiyah was back on track within a couple of weeks. With Afiyah's profound autism and learning difficulties, it took her a couple of weeks to get back to asking for the toilet by herself again, but for other children out there whose needs aren't as profound as Afiyah's, it may only take a few days or a week. If, for any reason, your child is taking longer to gain their toileting skills back, please don't panic.

I wish there was someone who could have told me that everything would be fine soon, but I didn't have anyone, and neither did I have the knowledge I now have. I only knew what I knew, and that was the fact that Afiyah's toileting skills were regressing.

The word upset is an understatement. I was devastated. Every time Afiyah had a wee accident at home, I used to hide away from her and cry – remember the rule of no commotions. But something within me had faith in the method I had created. I quickly went back to the basics and started using the timer again. I went right back to the start, and yes, it was heartbreaking to start again, but it worked. It worked quicker this time because Afiyah already knew what was happening, and I already had the experience of following all the steps.

I am mentioning this to prepare you so that you have the tools to deal with any setbacks. Just remember what you have done and know that the skills your child has learned can't disappear so easily. All the skills are still there, but there has been some cross-wiring because of someone accidentally verbally prompting them.

Speak with other family members, remind everyone of dos and don'ts, speak with the class teacher and TAs, and try to find out where and what might have gone wrong to have started this setback. Try and unpick as much as you can to find out what has triggered this setback so that you can avoid such triggers going forward. This whole process is one big behaviour plan, but the major difference here is that this behaviour plan teaches your child to use the toilet independently.

CHAPTER 8
Introducing Other Skills

For this chapter, let's say your child is 3 months into successfully using the toilet, and now is the time to start introducing other skills. Remember that I discouraged you from teaching your child other skills, such as cleaning themselves, undressing, dressing, flushing the toilet, washing hands, etc., whilst you were focusing on toilet training.

Now is the time to introduce one skill at a time and build on it.

1. Start with getting them to take their trousers and pants off to sit on the toilet. Now, if your child already knows how to do this, well done to both of you, but if your child doesn't, not a problem at all. For them to learn this skill independently, we'll have to go back to our basic skills, such as non-verbal prompts. Imagine your child is at the toilet, and they are expecting you to pull their trousers and pants to get them to sit on the toilet. At this moment, you will gently give your child a hand-over-hand approach – basically, you will hold their hands, place them on the trousers and help them to pull the trousers and pants down. I want you to maintain no eye contact and no speech. Don't tell them what to do. Just help them do it with a hand-over-hand approach. Before you know it, they will know

this process and will be able to undress their bottom half to sit on the toilet.

2. Use the same approach for wiping after having a wee. Give them some toilet paper in their hand and help them wipe clean. They will soon learn what to do and how to do it.

3. When it comes to teaching how to clean after a bowel movement, I would follow the same routine of a hand-over-hand approach. Afiyah has picked up on this to a certain extent, but she doesn't have any understanding of cleanliness. She has no concept of how clean she should be. She thinks just cleaning once will be enough, but sadly it's not, and I end up cleaning her after bowel movements. To be honest, with Afiyah we have the additional concern of urinary tract infections, which is why I have to intervene and ensure she is thoroughly cleaned. This may be a lot simpler for many other children out there compared to Afiyah's situation.

4. The same rule applies to getting dressed, flushing the toilet, and hand washing. Your new approach in life now is hand-over-hand support and no verbal prompts, and if you follow this, your children will be independent in no time.

Always remember our primary and most important goal is to get our children to understand their body, understand the sensation of a full bladder, develop bladder control, release bladder control only into the toilet, and have a poo into the toilet. If they learn other skills, such as cleaning themselves etc., then it's a bonus, but in this book, we are mainly focusing on connecting these dots in their mind, which will enable them to go to the toilet independently and without any prompts.

CHAPTER 9

What to do When You go Out?

Well, this is why I need you to read chapter 5 as well as other chapters. All chapters in this book are linked with one another. If you have skipped it, please go back and read it so that I can help you follow the steps for what to do when you go out.

1. You are about to leave the house – we generally get our toddlers to use the toilet as we are about to leave the house. This is what we are going to do with our autistic children, too. Doesn't matter how far along your child is in this toilet training program and doesn't matter how many months it has been for your child using the toilet independently. We will revert to using the timer when it's time to leave the house. Mainly because we want to avoid any verbal prompts.

2. Set the timer so that it goes off when you want. As soon as the timer goes off, your child will use the toilet, and you all leave the house straight after that. If you plan to be on the road for a while, try to limit fluid intake for only this period. We want to avoid wee/poo accidents at all costs, as now the new norm is to have a wee & poo into the toilet. Also, by this stage, your child

is having drinks at regular intervals throughout the day compared to the beginning of this program when you were offering drinks every 15 minutes.

3. Remember to take the timer every time you leave the house, since the timer is your new best friend now. Also, carry the 'toilet' and 'go' hand symbols with you. As soon as you reach your destination, I am sure you will look for where the toilets are. When you have located the toilet, set the timer to go off, show the toilet symbol to your child, get them to tap on the toilet symbol whilst you say the word "toilet", and guide them into the toilet. Remember the rule of 'no verbal prompts'.

4. Give them enough time on the toilet, and as soon as they have had a wee or a poo, reward them with their motivator No. 2. Of course, you also have this motivator with you everywhere you go.

5. Depending on your child's stage, set the timer accordingly and follow all the steps you have read in the previous chapters.

This is how you stay consistent with your approach wherever you are, and you are avoiding confusion for your child.

You will eventually reach a stage where your child will ask for the toilet without a timer even when you are out of the house. Always remember to have the 'toilet' symbol with you, though, so that it acts as a visual reminder for your child.

CHAPTER 10
What to Tell Your Child's School?

You go, "in your face, people, I have done what no professional has managed to achieve in years!"

Okay, this is clearly a joke and a bad one, too. If any professionals are reading this book, please take this as a joke, because that's what it is.

I have been a Specialist Teaching Assistant at an outstanding special school for several years, and with a hand on my heart, I can say all staff members work really hard, and if they had the resources or extra staffing, then no child would be in nappies. Sadly, that's not the case, and with the recent funding crisis, things seem to be getting worse, our teachers and TAs are thinly stretched, and hence I doubt schools will be able to toilet-train from scratch. However, once you have laid the groundwork, all teachers and TAs will be delighted to follow your plan.

This book is for parents, carers, and professionals, too. Other than asking the staff to buy & read this book, you can also write a list of strategies for the school to follow. Try and think from a teacher's point of view. There will be other children in the classroom. Your child could be in the middle of a lesson when they need a toilet. The plus point here is your child has been through at least 5-6 weeks of the toilet-training program with you, and now they know what to do.

Since I toilet-trained Afiyah during the summer break, I decided to make an appointment with the class teacher on one of the inset days. I was keen to speak to the teacher personally and pass on all the information before Afiyah started school. I talked about the steps and gave a copy of the strategies I felt they needed to implement in the classroom so that Afiyah could carry on with her new skills of asking for the toilet independently.

This is what I wrote, and you can use this for reference:

1. *When Afiyah arrives at school, guide her into the toilet before she gets to the classroom* – (this becomes the new routine for your child now. As soon as they get to their school, they go to the toilet first).

2. *No verbal prompts at any time please, especially when Afiyah is being guided into the toilet. Use the method of "invisible helper" to guide Afiyah into the toilet.* ("Invisible helper" is a term your child's class teachers and TAs should be familiar with. This basically means the person helping the child guides them from behind without using any verbal prompts/language).

3. *Use the timer at regular intervals throughout the day so that Afiyah uses that as a cue to go to the toilet.* (Give them the timer and tell them the importance of using it. Hence, I feel it's beneficial for teachers and other professionals to read this book to understand the depth of all the strategies you have put in place).

4. *Please NEVER verbally ask Afiyah to use the toilet. Always rely on the timer. If you are walking past a toilet on the way to the classroom or out of the school building, gently guide Afiyah into the toilet as an invisible helper.*

5. *Use the timer before Afiyah enters the playground and leaves the school building at the end of the day.*

- Make sure the class has enough 'toilet' symbols around the classroom and school. If not, request the class teacher to implement this before your child starts. Even if your child is verbal, having easy access to visual symbols will also benefit your child and the staff.

- Also, get the class teacher to implement 'toilet' symbols on small communication boards that can be carried around by your child's TAs around the playground and wherever they go. This will be a good visual reminder for your child without making any verbal prompts and your child will ask for the toilet when needed.

- Send a small basket of motivator No. 1 for the teacher to leave in the toilet closest to your child's class – let's hope they don't need their motivator No. 1 by this point, but it's best to have it handy in case they do.

- Most importantly, send in motivator No. 2 to your child's school. This is very important, and your child needs to know they are being rewarded for having a wee and poo into the toilet at school as well. After all, your child has learned the art of going to the toilet for this motivator, and it's imperative they get rewarded for this. I understand schools have healthy eating policies these days, and rightly so, but if you send in some sweets for only toilet-training purposes, I am sure the school will comply and be happy to support you. After all, schools want your child to be fully toilet-trained as well.

- Sending in your child's drink is also important. You want to ensure your child stays hydrated throughout the day and still understands the sensation of a full bladder. I am not saying you still have to give a drink every 15 mins – this was just for initial toilet-training purposes. By this stage, your child can have fluids at regular intervals of every hour or so.

By following these strategies, we are eliminating the chances of your child being unable to make it to the toilet in time if they are playing in the playground. Also, by making sure the school uses the timer to get your child to use the toilet before leaving the school building, we are again eliminating the possibility of your child needing a wee whilst there are on transport.

Before you know it, your child and the class teacher/TAs will get into their own routine of using the toilet effectively and positively to maintain all the hard work you have put in over the weeks.

Do's	Don'ts
Keep it positive	No reaction, no eye contact, no verbal talk when your child has wee/poo accidents. No commotion
Hand-over-hand approach	NO VERBAL PROMPTS
Regular drinks, keep track of fluid intake. Use the drink tracker provided.	Avoid foods with high salt content as this will absorb water, and your child's bladder won't get full easily.
Keep track of toilet visits, wees, poos, accidents, etc. Use the toilet-training data sheet provided.	Don't introduce other new skills. Only concentrate on toilet training for now. You can teach other skills once your child is confident about their toileting skills.
Use a timer to get them to the toilet, to get them to sit on the	NO VERBAL PROMPTS

toilet, and when you leave the house.	
Use the 'toilet' symbol to take them to the toilet and use the 'go' hand symbol to get them off the toilet seat.	NO VERBAL PROMPTS when you are taking them to the toilet. Only say the word "toilet" when your child taps on the symbol.
Use Motivator No. 1 to help them to be sat on the toilet seat for at least 2 minutes. Use Motivator No. 2 after successful wee and poo into the toilet.	Don't rush them off the toilet seat or force them to sit. If motivator No. 1 isn't working, try to find another motivator. If your child is losing interest in motivator No. 2 after a few days/weeks, then find another one.

This is it; we have reached the end of our toilet-training program. As you can see, it's not rocket science, and I am certain you already knew most of the strategies I have mentioned in this book. All I have done is put all the strategies into practice and broken them down into simple, easy-to-follow steps.

I would say, go back to the pages you have highlighted and read them again if you need to. Also, refer to the notes you have been making at the back of this book.

After I had successfully toilet-trained Afiyah, I remembered my late maternal grandma, Akhtar Sultana, telling me how she toilet-trained all 4 of her children from the age of 6 weeks onwards. When she told me back in 2006 during my visit to India, I didn't take much notice of it. I thought she was hinting that I should start toilet training my eldest.

If we imagine, back in the day when nappies didn't exist, what did people do? They used cloth nappies and didn't have a choice but to toilet-train their children at a young age. My grandma told me how she used a specific sound as an auditory cue to teach her babies to wee on command whilst she held them over a small potty. Now I know it's possible, and she was a genius. If she were alive, she would be so proud of me and the fact that I am mentioning her strategy in my first book.

Everything you need for a successful toilet-training program is in this book, with a list of things you will need prior to starting this program.

I want you to always remember that you, your health, and your well-being are very important. If you find this overwhelming, take a step back or a short break to gather your thoughts and start again. I know how challenging this can be, but I see it as short-term intensive training for long-term gain for your child, you, and your whole family.

Don't hesitate to get in touch with me through my Facebook page. I'll be more than happy to chat with you and brainstorm if you are stuck at any point. Scan the barcodes to access my Facebook pages and website if you are reading paper copies or click on the link for e-books.

It's recently dawned on me what we, as parents and carers of children with additional needs, go through. The struggles we go through are unreal, but we do it, and sadly, the abuse we suffer whilst struggling is also unreal. Over the years, I have been called all sorts of names for wanting to do the best for my children and fight for their rights. In all of this, I had forgotten to fight for my rights and the respect I deserve. In light of raising awareness about this, I wrote a short poem expressing what we go through and shared it on my Facebook page Living_with_Autism. This poem received huge responses from several other parents and carers who could relate to it.

So, here we go…

When you hear the news?

When you hear the news of autism or diagnosis of any disability, you suddenly become a carer and a nurse and yet the world calls you careless.

From having a "normal" life, you now have adaptions to make.

You leave your dreams behind and dedicate your life to help your child in the best way possible and yet the world calls you irrational.

Your research on your child's disability is beyond belief, you know all the medicines your child takes inside & out, you are the only expert on their behaviour & care plan, and yet the world says you can't have a say because you don't have a degree.

You spend hours fighting for your child's rights, and now you are not only their parent, carer, nurse but you also become their advocate and all you hear from the world is that you are being fussy and paranoid.

You block all the noises and do your best, but sometimes you are overwhelmed and at your most vulnerable times, the world calls you crazy.

Despite everything, you carry on because the only driving force is the love for your child and you suddenly become a warrior too.

So, when you are having a bad day, remember the numerous roles you play in your child's life and be proud of who you are.

Doesn't matter how small your child's progress is, it's there because of YOU.

So when you hear the world calling you names, remember what you really are and know your worth, because there is no one like YOU in this world.

Faria

References

Triad of Impairment

Andrew Cashin MHN, NP, Dip App Sci BHSC, GCert PTT, MN, PhD, Philip Barker RN, PhD, FRCN (2009). *The Triad of Impairment in Autism Revisited: Journal of Child and Adolescent Psychiatric Nursing/Volume 22, Issue 4/p.189-193.*

How long does it take to form a habit?

Phillippa Lally, Cornelia H. M. van Jaarsveld, Henry W. W. Potts, Jane Wardle (2009). *How are habits formed: European Journal of Social Psychology/Volume 40, Issue 6/p.998-1009.*

Notes

The contents of this book are based on my personal experience of toilet-training my autistic daughter and running toilet-training workshops. I am not a doctor and make no claim to dispense medical advice, healthcare advice or administer therapy. The training materials are intended to provide helpful and useful information on the subject addressed in this book. This method does not advocate corporal punishment or shaming of children. It's important to recognise that your child's particular diagnosis will be a huge part of his/her toilet training. For example, if your child has Oppositional Defiance Disorder, your child most likely will be defiant about the transition from nappies to toilet training strategies, and other disabilities may have different limitations beyond my knowledge and experience. The use of this toilet training method is at your discretion.

Printed in Great Britain
by Amazon